BREAKING STEREOTYPES

SEEING PEOPLE FOR WHO THEY ARE

VERNON J. DEFLANDERS

Table Of Content

INTRODUCTION

WELCOME TO BREAKING STEREOTYPES
SEEING PEOPLE FOR WHO THEY ARE!

Have you ever heard someone say something like, "You can't do that because you're a girl," or "People like you don't belong here"? Maybe you've noticed how certain characters in movies or TV shows always act a certain way because of how they look, where they're from, or what they believe. These are examples of stereotypes—fixed ideas about people that aren't always true and can often be harmful.

This book is here to help you understand what stereotypes are, why they exist, and how they affect people. But more importantly, it's here to show you how you can challenge stereotypes and make the world a kinder, more inclusive place.

Why This Book Matters

Stereotypes are everywhere. They show up in the things we watch, the things we hear, and even in the way we think about others. Sometimes, we don't even realize we're using stereotypes! But here's the thing: stereotypes can hurt people. They can make someone feel like they don't belong, like they're not good enough, or like they have to act a certain way just to fit in.

The good news? We can change this. By learning to recognize stereotypes and challenging them, we can create a world where everyone feels valued for who they truly are. And that's exactly what this book is all about.

What You'll Learn

In this book, you'll discover:
- What stereotypes are and where they come from.
- How stereotypes can hurt people and communities.
- How to recognize your own biases and challenge them.
- Ways to celebrate differences and appreciate diversity.
- Practical tools for standing up against stereotypes.
- How to create a more inclusive world, starting with your own actions.

Each chapter will guide you through these ideas with real-life examples, fun activities, and reflection questions to help you think about what you've learned.

Why You're Important

You might be wondering, "What can I do? I'm just one person." But here's the truth: you have the power to make a difference. Every time you choose to treat someone with kindness and respect, every time you stand up for what's right, and every time you challenge a stereotype, you're helping to create a better world.

This book is your guide, but you are the one who will make the change happen. You'll learn how to see people for who they really are—not just what others say about them. And in doing so, you'll inspire others to do the same.

How to Use This Book

This book is designed to be fun, interactive, and easy to follow. Here's how you can get the most out of it:

- **Take Your Time:** Read each chapter carefully and think about what it means to you.
- **Do the Activities:** Each chapter includes activities to help you practice what you've learned.
- **Reflect:** Use the reflection questions to think about your own experiences and how you can grow.
- **Share:** Talk about what you're learning with friends, family, or classmates. Sharing your thoughts can help others learn too!
- **Take Action:** Use the tools and strategies in this book to make a difference in your school, community, and beyond.

A Journey Worth Taking

By the time you finish this book, you'll have a better understanding of stereotypes and how to challenge them. You'll also have the tools to create a more inclusive world—one where everyone is seen and valued for who they truly are.

So, are you ready to get started? Let's dive in and begin this journey together. The world needs people like you to lead the way!

Chapter 1

WHAT ARE STEREOTYPES?

Understanding Stereotypes

Imagine you're meeting someone for the first time. Before they even say a word, you might already have an idea about who they are based on how they look, where they're from, or what they're wearing. This is something we all do—it's a natural part of how our brains work. But sometimes, these quick judgments are based on stereotypes.

A **stereotype** is a fixed idea or belief about a group of people. It's like putting everyone in a group into the same box, assuming they're all the same. For example:

- "Boys are better at sports than girls."
- "People who wear glasses are nerdy."
- "All teenagers are lazy."

These statements might sound familiar, but they're not true for everyone. Stereotypes oversimplify people and ignore their individuality.

Where Do Stereotypes Come From?

Stereotypes don't just appear out of nowhere. They come from many places, including:

- **Media:** Movies, TV shows, books, and advertisements often show people in stereotypical roles. For example, a superhero might always be a strong man, while a nurse is often shown as a caring woman.
- **Family and Friends**: Sometimes, the people around us pass down stereotypes without even realizing it. For example, a parent might say, "Boys don't cry," or a friend might joke, "You're so smart because you're Asian."
- **History and Culture:** Stereotypes can also come from historical events or cultural traditions. For example, certain groups might be labeled as "hardworking" or "dangerous" because of how they were treated in the past.
- **Personal Experiences:** If you meet one person from a group who acts a certain way, you might assume everyone in that group is the same.

It's important to remember that stereotypes are learned—they're not something we're born with. And because they're learned, they can also be unlearned.

Why Are Stereotypes Harmful?

At first, stereotypes might not seem like a big deal. But they can have serious consequences, such as:

- **Limiting People:** Stereotypes can make people feel like they have to act a certain way to fit in. For example, a boy who loves art might feel pressured to play sports instead because "boys are supposed to be athletic."

- **Hurting Feelings:** Stereotypes can make people feel misunderstood or invisible. For example, someone might feel hurt if others assume they're not smart just because of how they look.
- **Creating Barriers:** Stereotypes can lead to discrimination, where people are treated unfairly because of their race, gender, religion, or other characteristics.
- **Preventing Connection:** When we rely on stereotypes, we miss out on getting to know people for who they really are.

Breaking Down Stereotypes

The first step to breaking stereotypes is recognizing them. Here are some questions to ask yourself:

- Have I ever assumed something about someone without really knowing them?
- Where did that assumption come from? Was it something I saw, heard, or experienced?
- How might that assumption make the other person feel?

Once you start noticing stereotypes, you can challenge them. For example:

- If you hear someone say, "Girls aren't good at math," you can respond, "That's not true. I know lots of girls who are great at math!"
- If you catch yourself thinking, "He's probably not friendly because he looks serious," remind yourself to give the person a chance before making a judgment.

Activity: Spot the Stereotype

Take a moment to think about the last movie, TV show, or book you enjoyed. Write down the characters and their roles. Then, ask yourself:

- Did any of the characters fit into stereotypes?
- Were there any characters who broke stereotypes?
- How did those stereotypes affect the story?

This activity will help you start noticing stereotypes in the media you consume.

Reflection Questions

- Can you think of a time when someone made an assumption about you based on a stereotype? How did it make you feel?
- Have you ever made an assumption about someone else? What did you learn from that experience?
- Why do you think it's important to challenge stereotypes?

Key Takeaways

- Stereotypes are fixed ideas about groups of people that aren't always true.
- They come from media, family, culture, and personal experiences.
- Stereotypes can hurt people by limiting them, creating barriers, and preventing real connections.
- By recognizing and challenging stereotypes, we can see people for who they truly are.

In the next chapter, we'll explore how stereotypes affect individuals and communities—and what we can do to create a more inclusive world.

Chapter 2

HOW STEREOTYPES AFFECT US

The Power of Stereotypes

Stereotypes might seem like just words or ideas, but they can have a big impact on people's lives. Imagine being told over and over again that you're not good enough, that you don't belong, or that you have to act a certain way because of who you are. Over time, these messages can shape how people see themselves and how they interact with the world.

In this chapter, we'll explore how stereotypes affect individuals, communities, and even society as a whole. By understanding their impact, we can take steps to reduce their harm and create a more inclusive world.

How Stereotypes Affect Individuals

Stereotypes can influence how people think, feel, and behave. Here are some ways they can affect individuals:

- **Self-Doubt:** When people hear negative stereotypes about their group, they might start to believe them. For example, a girl who's told "girls aren't good at science" might feel less confident in her abilities, even if she's really talented.

- **Pressure to Conform:** Stereotypes can make people feel like they have to act a certain way to fit in. For example, a boy who loves dancing might feel pressured to play sports instead because "boys are supposed to be tough."

- **Missed Opportunities:** Stereotypes can limit what people think they can achieve. For example, someone might not apply for a job or try a new hobby because they believe it's "not for people like them."

- **Emotional Pain:** Being judged or treated unfairly because of a stereotype can hurt. It can make people feel invisible, misunderstood, or even ashamed of who they are.

How Stereotypes Affect Communities

Stereotypes don't just affect individuals—they also impact entire communities. Here's how:

- **Division:** Stereotypes can create "us vs. them" thinking, where people see others as different or less than. This can lead to prejudice, discrimination, and even conflict.

- **Inequality:** Stereotypes can contribute to unfair treatment in schools, workplaces, and other areas of life. For example, a teacher might assume a student isn't capable of succeeding because of their background, leading to fewer opportunities for that student.

- **Lack of Representation:** When stereotypes dominate, certain groups might not be represented fairly in media, leadership, or other spaces. This can make people feel like their voices don't matter.

How Stereotypes Affect Society

On a larger scale, stereotypes can shape how society functions. They can influence laws, policies, and cultural norms. For example:

- **Workplace Discrimination:** Stereotypes about gender, race, or age can affect who gets hired, promoted, or paid fairly.
- **Education Gaps:** Stereotypes about intelligence or ability can lead to unequal access to education and resources.
- **Social Injustice:** Stereotypes can contribute to systemic issues like racism, sexism, and other forms of discrimination.

When stereotypes go unchallenged, they can hold society back by preventing people from reaching their full potential.

Breaking the Cycle

The good news is that stereotypes don't have to define us. By recognizing their impact, we can take steps to break the cycle. Here's how:

- **Challenge Assumptions:** When you catch yourself thinking a stereotype, pause and ask, "Is this really true? Where did this idea come from?"
- **Speak Up:** If you hear someone using a stereotype, politely challenge them. For example, you could say, "I don't think that's true. Everyone is different."

- **Celebrate Diversity:** Learn about people from different backgrounds and appreciate what makes them unique. The more we understand each other, the less power stereotypes have.
- **Be a Role Model:** Show others how to treat people with kindness and respect. Your actions can inspire others to do the same.

Activity: Walk in Someone Else's Shoes

Think about a stereotype you've heard about a group of people. Then, imagine what it would feel like to be part of that group. Ask yourself:

- How would it feel to be judged based on that stereotype?
- What challenges might you face because of it?
- What would you want others to understand about you?

This activity can help you develop empathy and see the world from someone else's perspective.

Reflection Questions

- Can you think of a time when a stereotype affected you or someone you know? What happened?
- How do you think stereotypes affect your school, community, or society?
- What can you do to challenge stereotypes and create a more inclusive environment?

Key Takeaways

- Stereotypes can hurt individuals by causing self-doubt, limiting opportunities, and creating emotional pain.
- They can divide communities, create inequality, and lead to unfair treatment.

- On a larger scale, stereotypes can contribute to systemic issues in society.
- By challenging assumptions, speaking up, and celebrating diversity, we can reduce the harm caused by stereotypes.

In the next chapter, we'll dive into how we can recognize our own biases and take steps to overcome them. It's time to look inward and grow!

Chapter 3

RECOGNIZING AND OVERCOMING BIAS

What Is Bias?

Bias is like a lens through which we see the world. It's a preference or prejudice we have, often without even realizing it. Bias can influence how we think about people, situations, and even ourselves. While some biases are harmless (like preferring chocolate over vanilla), others can lead to unfair judgments and reinforce stereotypes.

There are two main types of bias:

- **Explicit Bias:** This is when we're aware of our preferences or prejudices. For example, someone might openly say, "I don't think women are good leaders."

- **Implicit Bias:** This is when we have unconscious attitudes or stereotypes that influence our actions. For example, someone might unknowingly assume that a man is more qualified for a job than a woman, even if their qualifications are the same.

Implicit bias is especially tricky because it happens automatically, without us realizing it. But the good news is that we can learn to recognize and challenge our biases.

Where Does Bias Come From?

Bias doesn't appear out of nowhere—it's something we learn over time. Here are some common sources of bias:

- **Family and Upbringing:** The beliefs and values we grow up with can shape how we see the world. For example, if a child hears their parents say, "People from that neighborhood are dangerous," they might grow up believing it.
- **Media:** Movies, TV shows, news, and social media often portray people in stereotypical ways, which can influence our perceptions.
- **Personal Experiences:** If we have a positive or negative experience with someone from a certain group, we might generalize that experience to everyone in that group.
- **Cultural Norms:** Society often teaches us what's "normal" or "acceptable," which can lead to biases against people who are different.

How to Recognize Your Own Biases

The first step to overcoming bias is recognizing it. Here are some ways to identify your biases:

- **Pay Attention to Your Thoughts:** Notice the assumptions you make about people. For example, do you assume someone is good at math because of their race? Or that someone is unfriendly because of how they look?
- **Reflect on Your Reactions:** Think about how you react to different people or situations. For example, do you feel more comfortable around certain groups of people? Why?
- **Ask for Feedback:** Sometimes, others can see our biases more clearly than we can. Ask a trusted friend or family member if they've noticed any biases in your behavior.
- **Take a Test:** There are online tools, like the Implicit Association Test (IAT), that can help you uncover hidden biases.

Recognizing bias isn't about feeling guilty—it's about being honest with yourself so you can grow.

How to Overcome Bias

Once you've identified your biases, you can take steps to overcome them. Here's how:

- **Educate Yourself:** Learn about people from different backgrounds, cultures, and experiences. The more you know, the less likely you are to rely on stereotypes.
- **Challenge Stereotypes:** When you catch yourself thinking a stereotype, replace it with a more accurate and positive thought. For example, instead of thinking, "Teenagers are lazy," remind yourself, "Not all teenagers are the same. Many are hardworking and passionate."
- **Practice Empathy:** Try to see the world from someone else's perspective. Ask yourself, "How would I feel if I were in their shoes?"

- **Build Relationships:** Spend time with people who are different from you. Personal connections can help break down biases and build understanding.
- **Be Open to Change:** Recognize that overcoming bias is a lifelong process. Be willing to admit when you're wrong and keep learning.

Activity: Bias Journal

For one week, keep a journal of your thoughts and reactions. Each day, write down:

- A situation where you made an assumption about someone.
- What that assumption was based on.
- Whether the assumption turned out to be true.
- How you could approach a similar situation differently in the future.

This activity will help you become more aware of your biases and take steps to challenge them.

Reflection Questions

- Can you think of a time when your bias influenced how you treated someone? What happened?
- How do you feel when someone makes an assumption about you based on a bias?
- What steps can you take to recognize and overcome your own biases?

Key Takeaways

- Bias is a preference or prejudice that can influence how we think and act.
- It can be explicit (conscious) or implicit (unconscious).

- Bias comes from family, media, personal experiences, and cultural norms.
- By recognizing and challenging our biases, we can treat people more fairly and build stronger connections.

In the next chapter, we'll explore how to create inclusive environments where everyone feels valued and respected. Together, we can make a difference!

Chapter 4

CREATING INCLUSIVE ENVIRONMENTS

What Does Inclusion Mean?

Inclusion is about making sure everyone feels valued, respected, and supported, no matter who they are. It's not just about tolerating differences—it's about celebrating them. An inclusive environment is one where people feel like they belong and can be their true selves without fear of judgment or discrimination.

In this chapter, we'll explore what it means to create inclusive spaces at school, work, and in our communities. We'll also look at practical steps we can take to make inclusion a reality.

Why Is Inclusion Important?

Inclusion benefits everyone. Here's why:

- **Fosters Belonging:** When people feel included, they're more likely to feel connected and supported. This leads to stronger relationships and communities.
- **Encourages Growth:** Inclusive environments expose us to new ideas, perspectives, and experiences, helping us grow as individuals.
- **Promotes Fairness:** Inclusion ensures that everyone has equal opportunities to succeed, regardless of their background or identity.
- **Boosts Creativity and Innovation:** When people from diverse backgrounds come together, they bring unique ideas and solutions to the table.

What Does an Inclusive Environment Look Like?

An inclusive environment is one where:

- Everyone feels safe to express themselves.
- Differences are respected and celebrated.
- People listen to and learn from each other.
- Discrimination, bullying, and exclusion are not tolerated.

For example, an inclusive classroom might have books and materials that reflect diverse cultures, abilities, and experiences. An inclusive workplace might have policies that support employees of all genders, races, and abilities.

How to Create Inclusive Environments

Creating an inclusive environment takes effort, but it's worth it. Here are some steps you can take:

- **Educate Yourself:** Learn about different cultures, identities, and experiences. The more you know, the better equipped you'll be to create an inclusive space.
- **Use Inclusive Language:** Be mindful of the words you use. For example, instead of saying "guys" to a group, try "everyone" or "folks."
- **Listen and Learn:** When someone shares their experiences, listen with an open mind. Avoid interrupting or making assumptions.
- **Challenge Exclusion:** If you see someone being excluded or treated unfairly, speak up. For example, if a classmate is being left out of a group project, invite them to join.
- **Celebrate Diversity:** Find ways to highlight and celebrate differences. For example, you could organize a cultural appreciation day or learn about holidays from different traditions.
- **Be Flexible:** Recognize that people have different needs and experiences. For example, a student with a disability might need extra time to complete an assignment, or a coworker might need a quiet space to work.

Activity: Inclusion in Action

Think about a space you're part of, like your school, workplace, or community. Ask yourself:

- Who feels included in this space?
- Who might feel left out?
- What changes could you make to ensure everyone feels welcome?

Then, take one small step to make that space more inclusive. For example, you could invite someone new to sit with you at lunch, or suggest adding more diverse books to your school library.

The Role of Leaders in Inclusion

Leaders play a big role in creating inclusive environments. Whether you're a teacher, manager, or community leader, you can set the tone for inclusion by:

- **Leading by example:** Show respect and kindness to everyone.
- **Setting clear expectations:** Make it clear that discrimination and exclusion won't be tolerated.
- **Providing resources:** Offer training, tools, and support to help others learn about inclusion.
- **Listening to feedback:** Be open to suggestions and ideas for improvement.

Even if you're not in a leadership role, you can still be a leader in inclusion by inspiring others through your actions.

Overcoming Challenges

Creating inclusive environments isn't always easy. You might face challenges like:

- Resistance from others who don't see the value of inclusion.
- Lack of resources or support.
- Your own biases or assumptions.

The key is to stay committed and keep learning. Remember, even small changes can make a big difference.

Reflection Questions

- Can you think of a time when you felt included? What made that experience special?

- Can you think of a time when you felt excluded? How did it affect you?
- What steps can you take to make your school, workplace, or community more inclusive?

Key Takeaways

- Inclusion is about creating spaces where everyone feels valued, respected, and supported.
- Inclusive environments benefit everyone by fostering belonging, encouraging growth, and promoting fairness.
- We can create inclusive spaces by educating ourselves, using inclusive language, listening to others, and celebrating diversity.
- Leaders play a key role in setting the tone for inclusion, but everyone can contribute to making a difference.

In the next chapter, we'll explore how to be an ally and support others in their journey toward inclusion and equality. Together, we can create a world where everyone feels like they belong.

Chapter 5

CELEBRATING DIFFERENCES

Diversity is Strength

The world is a rich tapestry of cultures, perspectives, and experiences. Each person brings something unique to the table, and it's this diversity that makes our communities, schools, and workplaces stronger. Celebrating differences isn't just about recognizing that people are different—it's about valuing those differences and understanding how they contribute to the greater good.

Here's why diversity is a strength:

- **New Perspectives:** People from different backgrounds see the world in unique ways. This leads to fresh ideas and creative solutions.

- **Stronger Communities:** When we embrace diversity, we build communities that are more inclusive, understanding, and supportive.
- **Personal Growth:** Learning about others helps us grow as individuals. It challenges our assumptions and broadens our horizons.
- **Global Connection:** In an increasingly connected world, understanding and appreciating diversity helps us work together across cultures and borders.

Think of diversity like a garden. A garden with just one type of flower might be pretty, but a garden with many different flowers is vibrant, colorful, and full of life. The same is true for our communities.

Learning from Others

One of the best ways to celebrate differences is to learn from others. Every person has a story to tell, and every culture has something valuable to teach us. By being curious and open-minded, we can discover new ways of thinking, living, and connecting.

Here are some ways to learn from others:

- **Ask Questions:** If someone is willing to share their experiences, ask thoughtful questions. For example, "What's a tradition that's important to your family?" or "What's something you love about your culture?"
- **Try New Things:** Step out of your comfort zone and try foods, music, or activities from different cultures. For example, you could attend a cultural festival or try cooking a dish from another country.
- **Listen to Stories:** Whether it's through books, movies, or conversations, stories are a powerful way to understand others' experiences.

- **Challenge Stereotypes:** If you catch yourself making assumptions about someone based on their background, pause and reflect. Remember, everyone is an individual with their own unique story.
- **Be Respectful:** When learning about others, approach the conversation with respect and humility. Avoid making judgments or comparisons.

By learning from others, we not only gain knowledge but also build empathy and understanding. We start to see the world through someone else's eyes, and that's a powerful thing.

Activity: Create a Diversity Collage

Let's celebrate differences through creativity! For this activity, you'll create a "diversity collage" that represents the beauty of diversity in your community or the world.

Instructions:

- Gather materials like magazines, newspapers, photos, or drawings.
- Look for images, words, or symbols that represent different cultures, perspectives, and experiences. For example, you might include pictures of traditional clothing, foods, or landmarks from around the world.
- Arrange your materials on a piece of paper or poster board to create a collage.
- Reflect on your collage. What does it say about the value of diversity? What did you learn while creating it?

If you prefer writing, you can also reflect on a time when you learned something new from someone different from you. What did they teach you? How did it change your perspective?

The Beauty of Differences

Celebrating differences doesn't mean ignoring what we have in common. It means recognizing that our shared humanity is enriched by our unique experiences and perspectives. When we embrace diversity, we create a world that is more vibrant, inclusive, and full of possibilities.

For example:

- A classroom with students from different backgrounds can learn from each other's traditions and stories.
- A workplace with employees from diverse cultures can come up with innovative ideas by combining their unique perspectives.
- A community that celebrates diversity can create events and spaces where everyone feels welcome and valued.

By celebrating differences, we create a world where everyone has a place and everyone's voice matters.

Reflection Questions

- What's something you've learned from someone who is different from you?
- How can you celebrate diversity in your school, workplace, or community?
- Why do you think diversity is important?

Key Takeaways

- Diversity is a strength that brings new perspectives, stronger communities, and personal growth.
- We can celebrate differences by learning from others, challenging stereotypes, and being open to new experiences.

- Activities like creating a diversity collage or reflecting on personal experiences can help us appreciate the beauty of diversity.

In the next chapter, we'll explore how to handle difficult conversations about bias, inclusion, and equality. These conversations can be challenging, but they're essential for growth and understanding.

Chapter 6

EMPTHY AND UNDERSTANDING

What is Empathy?

Empathy is the ability to understand and share the feelings of another person. It's about putting yourself in someone else's shoes and seeing the world from their perspective. Empathy is more than just feeling sorry for someone—it's about truly connecting with their emotions and experiences.

Empathy is important because:

- **It Builds Stronger Connections:** When we show empathy, we create deeper and more meaningful relationships.
- **It Reduces Conflict:** Understanding someone else's perspective can help resolve disagreements and prevent misunderstandings.

- **It Promotes Kindness:** Empathy encourages us to treat others with compassion and respect.
- **It Creates Inclusive Communities:** By understanding and valuing others' experiences, we can build environments where everyone feels seen and heard.

Empathy is a skill that can be developed with practice. It starts with listening, observing, and being open to understanding others.

Walking in Someone Else's Shoes

Practicing empathy means imagining what it's like to be in someone else's situation. It's about asking yourself, "How would I feel if I were in their place?" and responding with care and understanding.

Here are some ways to practice empathy in your daily life:

- **Listen Actively**
  - Pay attention when someone is speaking.
  - Avoid interrupting or thinking about what you'll say next.
  - Show that you're listening by nodding, making eye contact, and asking thoughtful questions.

- **Ask Questions**
  - If you don't understand someone's feelings or perspective, ask them.
  - For example, "How are you feeling about this?" or "What can I do to support you?"

- **Observe Nonverbal Cues**
  - Sometimes, people's body language or tone of voice can tell you how they're feeling.

- Look for signs like a slumped posture, a hesitant tone, or a forced smile.
- **Avoid Judging**
  - Everyone's experiences and emotions are valid.
  - Instead of judging or dismissing someone's feelings, try to understand where they're coming from.
- **Practice Kindness**
  - Small acts of kindness, like offering a helping hand or a kind word, can show empathy and make a big difference.
  - Reflect on Your Own Feelings
  - Think about times when you've felt sad, happy, frustrated, or excited.
  - Use those experiences to connect with others who might be feeling the same way.

Empathy doesn't mean you have to agree with someone or have all the answers. It's about showing that you care and that you're willing to understand their perspective.

Activity: Role-Playing Scenarios to Practice Empathy

Let's put empathy into action with a fun and interactive activity! Role-playing can help you practice empathetic responses in different situations.

Instructions:

- **Form Pairs or Small Groups**
  - If you're doing this activity alone, you can imagine the scenarios and write down your responses.
- **Choose a Scenario**
  - Here are some examples:

- A friend is upset because they didn't do well on a test.
- A classmate feels left out because they weren't invited to a party.
- A coworker is stressed about a big project deadline.
- A neighbor is worried about their sick pet.

- **Take Turns Role-Playing**
  - One person plays the role of the person in the scenario, and the other person practices responding with empathy.
  - **For example:**
    - Person A: "I'm so upset. I studied so hard for that test, but I still failed."
    - Person B: "I'm really sorry to hear that. It sounds like you worked really hard, and it must be so frustrating. Is there anything I can do to help?"

- **Reflect on the Experience**
  - After each role-play, discuss what went well and what could be improved.
  - How did it feel to give and receive empathy?

This activity helps you practice listening, understanding, and responding with care. It's a great way to build your empathy skills in a safe and supportive environment.

The Power of Empathy

Empathy has the power to transform relationships, communities, and even the world. When we take the time to understand and care for others, we create a ripple effect of kindness and connection.

For example:

- A teacher who shows empathy to a struggling student can inspire them to keep trying.
- A friend who listens with empathy can help someone feel less alone.
- A leader who practices empathy can create a workplace where everyone feels valued.

Empathy isn't just about helping others—it's also about growing as a person. When we practice empathy, we become more compassionate, understanding, and connected to the world around us.

Reflection Questions

- Can you think of a time when someone showed empathy to you? I low did it make you feel?
- How can you practice empathy in your daily life?
- Why do you think empathy is important for building strong relationships?

Key Takeaways

- Empathy is the ability to understand and share the feelings of others.
- Practicing empathy involves listening, asking questions, observing, and responding with kindness.
- Role-playing scenarios can help you develop your empathy skills.
- Empathy strengthens relationships, reduces conflict, and creates inclusive communities.

In the next chapter, we'll explore how to take action and make a positive impact in your community. Empathy is the foundation, but action is what brings change.

Chapter 7

RESPECTING EVERYONE

The Golden Rule

"Treat others the way you want to be treated." This simple yet powerful principle, known as the Golden Rule, is the foundation of respect. It reminds us to consider how our words and actions affect others and to treat everyone with kindness, fairness, and dignity—just as we would want to be treated.

Respect is about valuing people for who they are, regardless of their background, beliefs, or differences. It's not just about being polite; it's about recognizing the worth of every individual and showing them that they matter.

Why is respect important?

- **It Builds Trust:** Respect creates stronger, healthier relationships.

- **It Promotes Understanding:** When we respect others, we're more open to learning about their perspectives.
- **It Reduces Conflict**: Respectful behavior helps prevent misunderstandings and arguments.
- **It Creates a Positive Environment:** Whether at school, home, or in the community, respect makes everyone feel valued and included.

By practicing the Golden Rule, we can create a world where everyone feels respected and appreciated.

Respect in Action

Respect isn't just something we talk about—it's something we do. Here are some examples of how to show respect in different areas of your life:

1. At School

- **Listen to Others:** Pay attention when your teacher or classmates are speaking. Avoid interrupting or talking over them.
- **Be Inclusive:** Invite classmates to join your group or activity, especially if they seem left out.
- **Respect Differences:** Celebrate diversity by learning about your classmates' cultures, traditions, and perspectives.

2. At Home

- **Help Out:** Show respect for your family members by helping with chores or responsibilities.
- **Use Kind Words:** Speak to your siblings, parents, or guardians with kindness, even when you're upset.
- **Respect Privacy:** Knock before entering someone's room and respect their personal space.

3. **In the Community**

- Be Polite: Say "please," "thank you," and "excuse me" when interacting with others.
- Follow Rules: Respect community rules, like waiting your turn in line or keeping public spaces clean.
- Help Others: Offer assistance to neighbors, like carrying groceries or helping with yard work.

Respect is about treating everyone—friends, family, teachers, neighbors, and even strangers—with kindness and consideration. Small actions can make a big difference in showing others that you value and appreciate them.

Activity: How to Show Respect in Challenging Situations

Let's explore how to practice respect, even when it's difficult. This activity will help you think about respectful behavior in real-life situations.

Option 1: Group Discussion

- **Form a Circle:** Gather in a group and take turns sharing your thoughts.

- **Discuss Scenarios:**
  - What would you do if someone made fun of your friend?
  - How would you respond if you disagreed with someone's opinion?
  - What would you say if someone accidentally bumped into you and didn't apologize?

- **Share Ideas:** Talk about how to handle these situations respectfully. For example:
  - Instead of yelling or being rude, calmly explain how you feel.

- Listen to the other person's perspective, even if you don't agree.

Option 2: Worksheet

- **Write Down Scenarios:** Think of situations where showing respect might be challenging.
  - Example: A classmate takes your seat without asking.

- **Brainstorm Responses:** Write down how you could respond respectfully.
  - Example: Politely ask, "Could I have my seat back, please?"

- **Reflect:** Think about how your respectful response could improve the situation.

This activity helps you practice staying calm, kind, and respectful, even when faced with challenges. It's a great way to build your problem-solving and communication skills.

The Power of Respect

Respect is a two-way street. When we show respect to others, we're more likely to receive respect in return. It creates a positive cycle that strengthens relationships and builds a sense of community.

Here are some ways respect can make a difference:
- **In Friendships:** Respect helps friends feel valued and supported.
- **In Families:** Respect strengthens bonds and reduces conflicts.
- **In Communities:** Respect fosters cooperation and understanding among people from all walks of life.

Respect isn't always easy, especially when we're upset or frustrated. But choosing to act with respect, even in tough situations, shows strength and character. It's a skill that will serve you well throughout your life.

Reflection Questions

- Can you think of a time when someone showed you respect? How did it make you feel?
- How do you show respect to people who are different from you?
- What's one thing you can do to be more respectful in your daily life?

Key Takeaways

- Respect is about treating others the way you want to be treated.
- You can show respect by listening, being kind, and valuing others' differences.
- Respectful behavior creates trust, understanding, and positive relationships.
- Practicing respect, even in challenging situations, helps you grow as a person.

In the next chapter, we'll explore how to take action and make a positive impact in your community. Respect is the foundation, but action is what brings change.

Chapter 8

STANDING UP AGAINST STEREOTYPES

Being an Ally

Stereotypes are oversimplified ideas or assumptions about a group of people based on their race, gender, age, religion, or other characteristics. They can be harmful, unfair, and hurtful, often leading to discrimination and exclusion. Being an ally means standing up for others who are affected by stereotypes and working to create a more inclusive and fair environment.

What does it mean to be an ally?

- **Listen and Learn:** Take the time to understand the experiences of people who are affected by stereotypes. Listen to their stories and educate yourself about the challenges they face.

- **Show Support:** Let others know that you're there for them. A kind word or a simple "I'm here for you" can make a big difference.
- **Speak Up:** When you see or hear stereotypes being used, don't stay silent. Use your voice to challenge unfair assumptions and advocate for respect and equality.
- **Be Inclusive:** Make an effort to include everyone, regardless of their background or identity. Show that you value and respect diversity.
- **Be a Role Model:** Set an example by treating everyone with kindness and fairness. Your actions can inspire others to do the same.

Being an ally isn't about being perfect—it's about trying your best to support others and stand up against stereotypes. Even small actions can have a big impact.

Speaking Up

When you see or hear stereotypes, it's important to address them in a respectful and constructive way. Speaking up can help challenge harmful ideas and encourage others to think differently.

Here are some strategies for addressing stereotypes:

1. Ask Questions

- Sometimes, people don't realize they're using stereotypes. Asking questions can help them reflect on their words or actions.
  - Example: "What makes you think that?" or "Why do you believe that?"

2. Share Your Perspective

- Explain why the stereotype is harmful or unfair. Use "I" statements to express your feelings.
  - Example: "I feel uncomfortable when I hear that because it's not true for everyone."

3. Provide Facts

- Challenge stereotypes with accurate information.
  - Example: "Actually, that's a common misconception. Here's what I've learned…"

4. Be Calm and Respectful

- Avoid getting angry or confrontational. Stay calm and focus on having a constructive conversation.
  - Example: "I know you didn't mean to offend anyone, but that comment could be hurtful."

5. Offer an Alternative

- Suggest a more inclusive way of thinking or speaking.
  - Example: "Instead of saying that, maybe we could focus on what makes each person unique."

6. Know When to Walk Away

- If the person isn't willing to listen or change, it's okay to walk away. You've done your part by speaking up.

Speaking up against stereotypes can be challenging, but it's an important step toward creating a more respectful and inclusive world.

Activity: Practice Responding to Stereotypes

Let's practice standing up against stereotypes with a writing or role-playing activity. This will help you feel more confident and prepared to address stereotypes when you encounter them.

Option 1: Writing Activity

- **Think of a Scenario:** Imagine a situation where someone uses a stereotype.
  - Example: "Girls aren't good at sports."
- **Write a Response:** Write down how you would respond to challenge the stereotype.
  - Example: "That's not true. I know lots of girls who are amazing athletes."
- **Reflect:** Think about how your response could help change the conversation and encourage others to think differently.

Option 2: Role-Playing Activity

- **Form Pairs or Small Groups:** If you're doing this activity alone, you can imagine the scenarios and practice your responses out loud.
- **Choose a Scenario:** Take turns role-playing situations where stereotypes are used.
  - Example: Someone says, "Boys don't cry."
- **Practice Responding:** One person plays the role of the person using the stereotype, and the other person practices responding.
  - Example: "That's not true. Everyone has feelings, and it's okay to express them."
- **Switch Roles:** Take turns practicing different scenarios and responses.

Reflection Questions:

- How did it feel to respond to the stereotype?
- What worked well in your response?
- What could you do differently next time?

This activity helps you practice speaking up in a safe and supportive environment. It's a great way to build your confidence and communication skills.

The Power of Standing Up

When we stand up against stereotypes, we're not just helping individuals—we're creating a ripple effect that can change the way people think and act. Here's how standing up makes a difference:

- **It Challenges Harmful Ideas:** Speaking up helps break down stereotypes and replace them with understanding and respect.
- **It Empowers Others:** When you stand up, you inspire others to do the same.
- **It Creates Change:** By addressing stereotypes, we can build a more inclusive and fair society.

Remember, you don't have to do it alone. When we work together to challenge stereotypes, we can create a world where everyone is valued for who they are.

Reflection Questions

- Can you think of a time when you heard or saw a stereotype? How did it make you feel?
- How can you support someone who is affected by stereotypes?
- What's one thing you can do to challenge stereotypes in your daily life?

Key Takeaways

- Stereotypes are harmful assumptions about groups of people.
- Being an ally means supporting others and standing up against stereotypes.
- You can address stereotypes by asking questions, sharing your perspective, and staying calm and respectful.
- Practicing responses to stereotypes can help you feel more confident in real-life situations.

In the next chapter, we'll explore how to take action and make a positive impact in your community. Standing up against stereotypes is just the beginning—together, we can create a world where everyone is treated with fairness and respect.

Chapter 9

FRIENDSHIP WITHOUT BOUNDARIES

Building Inclusive Friendships

Friendship is one of the most beautiful connections we can have in life. It brings joy, support, and understanding. But sometimes, we limit ourselves by only forming friendships with people who are similar to us. Building inclusive friendships means opening our hearts and minds to people from different backgrounds, cultures, and experiences.

Why are inclusive friendships important?

- **They Broaden Your Perspective:** Friends from different backgrounds can teach you new ways of thinking and help you see the world through their eyes.

- **They Celebrate Diversity:** Inclusive friendships show us that our differences make us unique and special.
- **They Build Empathy:** Getting to know someone who is different from you helps you understand and appreciate their experiences.
- **They Create Stronger Communities:** When we form friendships without boundaries, we help build a world where everyone feels valued and included.

Friendship knows no boundaries. It's not about where someone comes from, what they look like, or what they believe—it's about kindness, trust, and connection. By forming inclusive friendships, we can create a more compassionate and united world.

Breaking Barriers

Sometimes, we hesitate to befriend people who are different from us because of fears or misconceptions. These barriers can prevent us from forming meaningful connections. Let's address some common concerns and how to overcome them:

1. "What if we don't have anything in common?"

Solution: Focus on what you do have in common. Maybe you both enjoy the same hobbies, like the same music, or share similar goals. Even if your interests are different, you can learn from each other and discover new things together.

2. "What if I say or do the wrong thing?"

Solution: It's okay to make mistakes as long as you're respectful and willing to learn. If you're unsure about something, ask questions in a kind and open way. Most people appreciate your effort to understand them better.

3. **"What if they don't want to be friends with me?"**

Solution: Not everyone will become your best friend, and that's okay. But you'll never know unless you try. Start with a simple conversation or a kind gesture, and see where it leads.

4. **"What if others judge me for being friends with someone different?"**

Solution: True friendship is about valuing people for who they are, not what others think. Be proud of your inclusive friendships and set an example for others to follow.

5. **"What if we don't understand each other?"**

Solution: Communication is key. Be patient and open-minded, and take the time to learn about each other's perspectives. Understanding grows with time and effort.

Breaking barriers takes courage, but the rewards are worth it. Inclusive friendships enrich our lives and help us grow as individuals.

Activity: Friendship Challenge

Let's put what we've learned into action with a fun and meaningful challenge. This activity will help you build new connections or strengthen existing ones.

Option 1: Make a New Friend

- **Step Out of Your Comfort Zone:** Look for someone you don't know well, such as a classmate, neighbor, or teammate.

- **Start a Conversation:** Introduce yourself and ask questions to get to know them better.
  - Example: "What's your favorite hobby?" or "What do you like to do for fun?"

- **Find Common Ground:** Look for shared interests or experiences.

- **Plan an Activity:** Invite them to join you for something fun, like playing a game, working on a project, or sharing a meal.

Option 2: Learn Something New About an Existing Friend

- **Ask Deeper Questions:** Go beyond surface-level topics and learn more about your friend's background, culture, or experiences.
  - Example: "What's a tradition your family celebrates?" or "What's something you've always wanted to try?"

- **Share Your Own Story:** Open up about your own experiences and traditions.

- **Celebrate Your Differences:** Talk about what makes each of you unique and how those differences make your friendship special.

Reflection Questions:

- What did you learn about your new or existing friend?
- How did it feel to connect with someone in a deeper way?
- What can you do to continue building your friendship?

This challenge is a great way to practice forming inclusive friendships and appreciating the diversity around you.

The Power of Friendship Without Boundaries

Friendship is a bridge that connects people from all walks of life. When we form friendships without boundaries, we create a world where everyone feels seen, heard, and valued. Here's how inclusive friendships make a difference:

- **They Break Down Stereotypes:** Getting to know someone personally helps us see beyond stereotypes and appreciate them for who they truly are.
- **They Build Understanding:** Inclusive friendships teach us to respect and celebrate differences.
- **They Spread Kindness:** When we treat others with kindness and acceptance, we inspire others to do the same.

Remember, friendship is about connection, not perfection. It's okay to make mistakes or feel unsure at times. What matters most is your willingness to learn, grow, and build meaningful relationships.

Reflection Questions

- Can you think of a time when you made a friend who was different from you? What did you learn from them?
- What's one thing you can do to make someone feel included?
- How can you encourage others to form inclusive friendships?

Key Takeaways

- Inclusive friendships help us grow, learn, and celebrate diversity.
- Breaking barriers requires courage, but it leads to meaningful connections.
- Building friendships without boundaries creates a more compassionate and united world.
- Small actions, like starting a conversation or asking thoughtful questions, can lead to lasting friendships.

In the next chapter, we'll explore how to take the lessons we've learned and turn them into actions that make a positive impact in our communities. Friendship without boundaries is just the beginning—together, we can create a world where everyone feels connected and valued.

Chapter 10

CELEBRATING INDIVIDUALITY

Uniqueness is Beautiful

Imagine a world where everyone was exactly the same—same thoughts, same looks, same talents. It would be pretty boring, wouldn't it? What makes the world vibrant and exciting is the fact that each of us is unique. Our individuality is what makes us special, and it's something to be celebrated.

Why is individuality important?

- **It Defines Who You Are:** Your personality, talents, and experiences make you one of a kind. There's no one else in the world exactly like you!

- **It Inspires Others:** When you embrace your individuality, you encourage others to do the same.

- **It Creates Diversity:** Our differences make the world richer and more interesting.
- **It Builds Confidence:** Loving who you are helps you feel strong and self-assured.

How can you celebrate your individuality?

- Focus on your strengths and talents.
- Be proud of your quirks and unique traits.
- Surround yourself with people who appreciate you for who you are.
- Celebrate the individuality of others by recognizing and respecting their differences.

Remember, your individuality is your superpower. Embrace it, celebrate it, and let it shine!

Overcoming Peer Pressure

Sometimes, it can be hard to stay true to yourself, especially when you feel pressure to fit in or be like everyone else. Peer pressure can make you question your choices, values, or even your identity. But staying true to yourself is one of the most important things you can do

What is peer pressure ?

Peer pressure is when you feel influenced to do something because others are doing it, or because you want to be accepted by a group. It can be positive (encouraging you to try something new) or negative (pushing you to do something that doesn't feel right).

How can you overcome negative peer pressure?

Know Your Values: Think about what's important to you and what makes you happy. Use these values as a guide for your decisions.

- **Be Confident in Who You Are:** Remind yourself that you don't need to change to fit in. The right friends will accept you for who you are.

- **Practice Saying No:** It's okay to say no to things that don't align with your values or make you uncomfortable.
  - Example: "Thanks, but that's not for me."

- **Find Supportive Friends:** Surround yourself with people who respect your individuality and encourage you to be yourself.

- **Be Respectful of Others:** While staying true to yourself, remember to respect the choices and individuality of others.

Overcoming peer pressure takes courage, but it's worth it. When you stay true to yourself, you'll feel happier, more confident, and more authentic.

Activity: Write a "Self-Celebration" Letter

Let's take a moment to celebrate YOU! This activity will help you reflect on your unique qualities and appreciate everything that makes you special.

Instructions:

- **Find a Quiet Space:** Take a few minutes to sit down with a pen and paper or a digital device.

- **Write a Letter to Yourself:** Pretend you're writing to a close friend—except this time, the friend is YOU!

- **Highlight Your Unique Qualities:** Think about what makes you special. This could include your talents, personality traits, accomplishments, or even your quirks.
  - Example: "I love how creative I am. I always come up

with fun ideas, and I'm proud of my ability to think outside the box."

- **Celebrate Your Growth:** Reflect on how far you've come and the challenges you've overcome.
    - Example: "I'm proud of how I stayed true to myself when I felt pressured to change. It wasn't easy, but I did it!"

- **End with Encouragement:** Write a few words of encouragement to remind yourself to keep embracing your individuality.
    - Example: "Keep being you, because the world needs your unique light!"

Reflection Questions:

- How did it feel to write about your unique qualities?
- What did you learn about yourself through this activity?
- How can you continue to celebrate your individuality every day?

This letter is a reminder of how amazing you are. Keep it somewhere safe, and read it whenever you need a boost of confidence or a reminder of your worth.

The Power of Celebrating Individuality

When we celebrate our individuality, we create a world where everyone feels valued and accepted. Here's why celebrating individuality matters:

- **It Builds Self-Love:** Embracing who you are helps you feel confident and happy in your own skin.
- **It Encourages Acceptance:** When we celebrate our own uniqueness, we're more likely to appreciate and respect the individuality of others.

- **It Fosters Creativity:** Our differences inspire new ideas, perspectives, and solutions.
- **It Strengthens Relationships:** Authenticity helps us form deeper, more meaningful connections with others.

Remember, you are enough just as you are. Your individuality is a gift to the world, and it deserves to be celebrated every single day.

Reflection Questions

- What are three things that make you unique?
- How can you celebrate your individuality in your daily life?
- How can you encourage others to embrace and celebrate their own uniqueness?

Key Takeaways

- Your individuality is what makes you special—embrace it and celebrate it.
- Overcoming peer pressure helps you stay true to yourself while respecting others.
- Writing a "self-celebration" letter is a great way to reflect on your unique qualities and build self-confidence.
- Celebrating individuality creates a more accepting, creative, and connected world.

In the next chapter, we'll explore how to take everything we've learned and turn it into action. By celebrating individuality, standing up against stereotypes, and building inclusive friend-ships, we can make a positive impact in our communities and beyond.

Chapter 11

LEARNING FROM MISTAKES

Mistakes Happen

Nobody is perfect. No matter how hard we try, we all make mistakes—it's a natural part of being human. Mistakes can feel frustrating or embarrassing, but they're also opportunities to learn and grow. Instead of fearing mistakes, we should embrace them as valuable life lessons.

Why are mistakes important?

- **They Help Us Learn:** Mistakes show us what doesn't work and help us figure out what does.
- **They Build Resilience:** Overcoming mistakes teaches us how to bounce back and keep going.

- **They Encourage Growth:** Each mistake is a chance to improve and become better.
- **They Make Us Human:** Mistakes remind us that it's okay to be imperfect.

How can we handle mistakes in a healthy way?

- Acknowledge the Mistake: Accept that it happened instead of ignoring or denying it.
- Learn from It: Ask yourself, "What can I do differently next time?"
- Move Forward: Don't dwell on the mistake—use it as motivation to grow.

Remember, making mistakes doesn't define you. What matters is how you respond to them. Every mistake is a stepping stone on the path to success.

Apologizing and Growing

When our mistakes affect others, it's important to take responsibility and make things right. Apologizing sincerely shows that we care about the feelings of others and are willing to grow from the experience.

How to Apologize Sincerely

- **Acknowledge What Happened:** Be honest about your mistake and take responsibility for it.
  - Example: "I realize I hurt your feelings when I said that."

- **Express Genuine Regret:** Let the other person know you're truly sorry.
  - Example: "I'm really sorry for what I did."

- **Make Amends:** Ask how you can make things better or take steps to fix the situation.
  - Example: "What can I do to make it up to you?"
- **Commit to Change:** Show that you're willing to learn from the mistake and do better in the future.
  - Example: "I'll make sure to think before I speak next time."

Why is apologizing important?

- It rebuilds trust and strengthens relationships.
- It shows maturity and accountability.
- It helps both you and the other person move forward.

Apologizing isn't always easy, but it's a powerful way to grow and show respect for others. Remember, everyone makes mistakes—it's how we handle them that truly matters.

Activity: Reflect on a Mistake

Let's take some time to reflect on a mistake you've made and think about how you can handle similar situations better in the future. This activity will help you turn a past mistake into a valuable learning experience.

Instructions:

- **Think About a Mistake:** Choose a mistake you've made in the past. It could be something small, like forgetting to do a task, or something bigger, like hurting someone's feelings.
- **Answer These Questions:**
  - What happened?
  - How did it make you feel?
  - How did it affect others?

- What did you learn from the experience?
- What would you do differently if it happened again?

- **Write Down Your Thoughts:** Use a journal, notebook, or digital device to write about your reflection. Be honest with yourself and focus on what you've learned.

Example Reflection:

- What happened? I forgot to include my friend in a group activity, and they felt left out.
- How did it make me feel? I felt bad for hurting their feelings and realized I wasn't being thoughtful.
- How did it affect others? My friend felt excluded and upset.
- What did I learn? I learned the importance of being inclusive and paying attention to how my actions affect others.
- What would I do differently? Next time, I'll make sure to invite everyone and double-check that no one feels left out.

Reflection Questions:

- How did reflecting on your mistake make you feel?
- What steps can you take to avoid making the same mistake again?
- How can you use this experience to grow and improve?

This activity is a great way to turn mistakes into opportunities for growth. By reflecting on what happened and planning for the future, you can handle similar situations with confidence and care.

The Power of Learning from Mistakes

Mistakes are not failures—they're lessons in disguise. When we embrace our mistakes and learn from them, we become stronger, wiser, and more compassionate. Here's why learning from mistakes is so powerful:

- **It Builds Self-Awareness:** Reflecting on mistakes helps us understand ourselves better.
- **It Encourages Growth:** Each mistake is a chance to improve and become a better version of ourselves.
- **It Strengthens Relationships:** Apologizing and making amends shows others that we value them and are willing to grow.
- **It Teaches Resilience:** Learning from mistakes helps us bounce back and keep moving forward.

Remember, mistakes are a natural part of life. They don't define you—they shape you. By learning from them, you can turn challenges into opportunities and become the best version of yourself.

Reflection Questions

- Can you think of a time when you learned something valuable from a mistake?
- How do you usually respond when you make a mistake?
- What steps can you take to handle mistakes in a positive way?

Key Takeaways

- Mistakes are a normal part of life and an opportunity to learn and grow.
- Apologizing sincerely and taking responsibility shows maturity and respect for others.
- Reflecting on past mistakes helps us handle similar situations better in the future.
- Learning from mistakes builds resilience, self-awareness, and stronger relationships.

In the next chapter, we'll explore how to take the lessons we've learned from mistakes and use them to create positive change in our lives and communities. Remember, every mistake is a stepping stone on the journey to becoming your best self.

Chapter 12

CREATING A MORE INCLUSIVE WORLD

Small Actions, Big Impact

Creating a more inclusive world might sound like a big task, but it starts with small, everyday actions. Inclusivity means making sure everyone feels valued, respected, and accepted for who they are. It's about celebrating differences and ensuring that no one feels left out.

Why do small actions matter?

- **They Create Ripple Effects:** A kind word or inclusive gesture can inspire others to do the same.

- **They Build a Culture of Belonging:** Small actions, when done consistently, create an environment where everyone feels welcome.They Show Empathy: Simple acts of understanding and kindness can make a big difference in someone's life.

Examples of Small Actions That Promote Inclusivity:

- **Listen to Others:** Take the time to hear people's stories and perspectives.
- **Use Inclusive Language:** Be mindful of the words you use and avoid stereotypes.
- **Invite Others to Join:** If you see someone sitting alone or feeling left out, invite them to join your group.
- **Stand Up for Others:** Speak up if you see someone being treated unfairly or excluded.
- **Celebrate Differences:** Show interest in other cultures, traditions, and experiences.

Inclusivity doesn't require grand gestures. It's the small, consistent actions that create a big impact over time. By being kind, open-minded, and respectful, you can help make the world a more inclusive place.

Be the Change

As the saying goes, "Be the change you wish to see in the world." If you want to live in a more inclusive world, it starts with you. By taking initiative and leading by example, you can inspire others to join you in promoting inclusivity.

How can you be the change?

- **Educate Yourself:** Learn about different cultures, identities, and experiences. The more you know, the better you can understand and support others.

- **Challenge Stereotypes:** Speak up when you hear stereotypes or assumptions about others.
  - Example: "Actually, that's not true. Everyone is different, and we shouldn't generalize."
- **Create Safe Spaces:** Make sure your school, community, or friend group is a place where everyone feels welcome and accepted.
- **Be a Role Model:** Show others what inclusivity looks like through your actions.
- **Encourage Others:** Inspire your friends, family, and classmates to join you in promoting inclusivity.

Examples of Taking Initiative:

- Organize a cultural appreciation day at school.
- Start a club or group focused on inclusivity and diversity.
- Volunteer with organizations that support marginalized communities.
- Share positive messages about inclusivity on social media.

Being the change doesn't mean you have to do everything on your own. It's about taking the first step and inspiring others to follow. Together, we can create a world where everyone feels valued and included.

Activity: Create a Personal Action Plan

Now it's time to take action! This activity will help you create a personal plan for promoting inclusion and challenging stereotypes in your daily life.

Instructions:

- **Reflect on Your Values:** Think about why inclusivity is important to you and what kind of world you want to help create.

- **Identify Areas for Change:** Look at your school, community, or friend group. Are there ways to make these spaces more inclusive?

- **Set Goals:** Write down 2-3 specific actions you can take to promote inclusivity.
  - Example: "I will invite someone new to sit with me at lunch."
  - Example: "I will learn about a culture I'm unfamiliar with and share what I learn with my friends."

- **Plan for Challenges:** Think about any obstacles you might face and how you can overcome them.
  - Example: "If someone makes a negative comment, I'll respond calmly and explain why inclusivity matters."

- **Take Action:** Start putting your plan into practice and track your progress.

Template for Your Action Plan:

Why Inclusivity Matters to Me: (Write a sentence or two about why you care about creating a more inclusive world.)

My Goals:

- (Write your first goal here.)
- (Write your second goal here.)
- (Optional: Write a third goal here.)

Challenges and Solutions:

- **Challenge:** (Write a potential challenge here.)
- **Solution:** (Write how you'll handle it.)
- **How I'll Take Action:** (Write a few steps you'll take to achieve your goals.)

Reflection Questions:

- How do you feel about your action plan?
- What impact do you hope to make with your actions?
- How can you encourage others to join you in promoting inclusivity?

This action plan is your guide to making a difference. Remember, even small steps can lead to big changes. By taking action, you're helping to create a world where everyone feels valued and included.

The Power of Inclusivity

Inclusivity isn't just about accepting others—it's about celebrating them. When we create a world where everyone feels valued, we all benefit. Here's why inclusivity is so powerful:

- **It Builds Stronger Communities:** Inclusivity brings people together and fosters a sense of belonging.
- **It Encourages Creativity:** Diverse perspectives lead to new ideas and solutions.
- **It Promotes Understanding:** Inclusivity helps us see the world through others' eyes and develop empathy.
- **It Makes the World Better:** When everyone feels valued, we create a kinder, more compassionate world.

Remember, you have the power to make a difference. By taking small actions and inspiring others, you can help create a world where everyone feels seen, heard, and respected.

Reflection Questions

- What does inclusivity mean to you?
- What small actions can you take to promote inclusivity in your daily life?

- How can you inspire others to join you in creating a more inclusive world?

Key Takeaways

- Small, everyday actions can have a big impact on creating a more inclusive world.
- Being the change means taking initiative and leading by example.
- A personal action plan can help you set goals and take steps to promote inclusivity.
- Inclusivity builds stronger communities, encourages creativity, and makes the world a better place.

In the next chapter, we'll explore how to take everything we've learned and turn it into a lifelong commitment to kindness, growth, and positive change. Remember, the journey to a more inclusive world starts with you.

CONCLUSION

YOUR JOURNEY TO GROWTH AND KINDNESS

Recap: What We've Learned

As we come to the end of this book, let's take a moment to reflect on the journey we've been on together. Throughout these chapters, we've explored important lessons about kindness, growth, and making a positive impact on the world around us.

Here are some of the key takeaways:

- **Kindness is Powerful:** Small acts of kindness can create big changes in the lives of others and in your own life.
- **Empathy Builds Bridges:** Understanding and respecting others' feelings and perspectives is the foundation of strong relationships.
- **Mistakes Are Opportunities:** Every mistake is a chance to learn, grow, and become better.
- **Inclusivity Matters:** Small, everyday actions can help create a world where everyone feels valued and accepted.
- **You Have the Power to Make a Difference:** By taking initiative and leading by example, you can inspire others and create positive change in your community.

Each chapter has been a step toward becoming the best version of yourself—someone who is kind, empathetic, resilient, and inclusive. These lessons are tools you can carry with you for the rest of your life.

Call to Action: Keep Growing

This book is just the beginning of your journey. Now it's time to take what you've learned and put it into action. Here's how you can continue growing and making a difference:

- **Practice What You've Learned:** Apply the lessons from this book in your daily life. Be kind, empathetic, and inclusive in everything you do.
- **Set Goals for Growth:** Think about the kind of person you want to be and set goals to help you get there.
- **Inspire Others:** Share what you've learned with your friends, family, and community. Encourage them to join you in creating a kinder, more inclusive world.
- **Keep Learning:** Growth is a lifelong journey. Stay curious, open-minded, and willing to learn from every experience.

Remember, change doesn't happen overnight. It's the small, consistent actions you take every day that lead to big, meaningful change. You have the power to make a difference—one step at a time.

Words of Encouragement

As you move forward, know this: You are capable of amazing things. You have the strength to overcome challenges, the courage to stand up for what's right, and the kindness to make the world a better place.

The world needs people like you—people who care, who listen, and who take action. Every small act of kindness, every moment of empathy, and every effort to include others makes a difference.

Are you gonna be in much longer don't worry about it take your time it knowledge those allegations alongside the announcingYou might not always see the impact right away, but trust that your actions are creating ripples of positivity that will spread far and wide.

When things get tough, remember:

- **You are resilient:** Mistakes and setbacks are part of the journey. Learn from them and keep moving forward.
- **You are enough:** Just by being yourself, you have the power to make a difference.
- **You are not alone:** There are others out there who share your vision for a kinder, more inclusive world. Together, you can create real change.

Believe in yourself and your ability to grow, inspire, and lead. The journey ahead is full of opportunities to learn, connect, and make a positive impact. You've already taken the first step by reading this book—now it's time to take the next step and put these lessons into action.

Final Thoughts

Thank you for joining me on this journey. I hope this book has inspired you to be kinder, more empathetic, and more inclusive in your daily life. Remember, the world is a better place because of people like you—people who care, who listen, and who take action to make a difference.

As you go forward, keep these words in mind:

- **Be kind:** To yourself and to others.
- **Be brave:** Stand up for what's right, even when it's hard.
- **Be the change:** Take small steps every day to create the world you want to live in.

You have the power to make a difference. The world is waiting for your light—go out there and shine.

This is not the end of your journey—it's just the beginning. Keep growing, keep learning, and keep making the world a better place. You've got this!

Additional Resources and References

To continue your journey of growth, kindness, and inclusivity, here are some additional resources to explore. These books, websites, and activities will help you deepen your understanding and take further steps toward making a positive impact in your life and community.

Books and Articles

"Wonder" by R.J. Palacio

- A heartwarming story about kindness, empathy, and acceptance, told through the eyes of a boy with facial differences.

"The Power of Kindness: The Unexpected Benefits of Leading a Compassionate Life" by Piero Ferrucci

- This book explores how kindness can transform your life and the lives of those around you.

"The Art of Empathy: A Complete Guide to Life's Most Essential Skill" by Karla McLaren

- A practical guide to understanding and practicing empathy in your daily life.

"Stamped: Racism, Antiracism, and You" by Jason Reynolds and Ibram X. Kendi

- A powerful exploration of racism and how to challenge it, written for young readers.

"Dare to Lead" by Brené Brown

- A guide to courageous leadership, focusing on empathy, vulnerability, and inclusivity.

"You Are Enough: A Book About Inclusion" by Margaret O'Hair and Sofia Sanchez

- A beautifully illustrated children's book that celebrates diversity and self-acceptance.

"How to Be an Antiracist" by Ibram X. Kendi

- A thought-provoking book that challenges readers to actively work toward a more inclusive and equitable world.

Articles:

- The Science of Kindness" by Greater Good Science Center
- "How to Teach Kids About Empathy" by PBS Parents
- "The Importance of Diversity and Inclusion in Schools" by Edutopia

Websites and Organizations

Greater Good Science Center
Website: https://greatergood.berkeley.edu

- A resource for research-based practices to promote kindness, empathy, and well-being.

Teaching Tolerance (Now Learning for Justice)
Website: https://www.learningforjustice.org

- Offers free resources for educators and students to promote diversity, equity, and inclusion.

Random Acts of Kindness Foundation
Website: https://www.randomactsofkindness.org

- Provides ideas, stories, and resources to inspire kindness in everyday life.

DoSomething.org
Website: https://www.dosomething.org

- A global organization that empowers young people to take action on social issues, including inclusivity and diversity.

UNICEF Voices of Youth

Website: https://www.voicesofyouth.org

- A platform for young people to share their perspectives and take action on global issues.

The Empathy Lab

Website: https://www.empathylab.uk

- Focuses on using stories to build empathy and understanding in children and young people.

Anti-Defamation League (ADL)

Website: https://www.adl.org

- Offers resources to combat hate and promote inclusivity and respect.

Inclusive Schools Network

Website: https://inclusiveschools.org

- Provides tools and strategies for creating inclusive school environments.

Activities and Worksheets

- **Personal Action Plan Template**
  - Create your own action plan for promoting inclusivity and challenging stereotypes.
  - Downloadable PDF: Personal Action Plan Template
- **Kindness Challenge Worksheet**
  - A fun activity to track your daily acts of kindness and reflect on their impact.
  - Downloadable PDF: Kindness Challenge Worksheet

- **Empathy Map Activity**
  - A printable worksheet to help you understand others' perspectives by mapping their feelings, thoughts, and experiences.
  - Downloadable PDF: Empathy Map Activity
- **Diversity Bingo**
  - A group activity to celebrate differences and learn about others in a fun, interactive way.
  - Downloadable PDF: Diversity Bingo
- **Stereotype Reflection Worksheet**
  - A guided worksheet to help you identify and challenge stereotypes in your thinking.
  - Downloadable PDF: Stereotype Reflection Worksheet
- **Inclusivity Poster Design**
  - Create a poster that promotes inclusivity and share it with your school or community.
  - Downloadable PDF: Inclusivity Poster Template
- **Gratitude Journal**
  - A printable journal to reflect on the things you're grateful for and how you can spread positivity to others.
  - Downloadable PDF: Gratitude Journal

- **Role-Playing Scenarios**
  - Practice responding to situations involving exclusion, bullying, or stereotypes through role-playing.
  - Downloadable PDF: Role-Playing Scenarios

Final Note

These resources are here to support you as you continue your journey of growth, kindness, and inclusivity. Whether you're reading a book, exploring a website, or completing an activity, remember that every step you take brings you closer to creating a better world for yourself and others.

Keep learning, keep growing, and keep making a difference!